HOW TO IMPROVE AT RESILIENCE IN 30 MINUTES

The Best Advice You Could Ever Get about RESILIENCE

Rosalie B Harlan

Table of Contents

INTRODUCTION

The ability to bounce back from challenging life situations is how resilience is often characterized.

Being resilient is not like bouncing up and down on a trampoline. It's more like trying to scale a mountain without a map. You'll probably encounter obstacles along the road, but patience, perseverance, and support from those around you are all necessary. But once you get there, you can see how far you've traveled and glance back.

CHAPTER 1:

RESILIENCE

Adversity comes in many different forms for people throughout life. Personal experiences might include things like disease, the death of a loved one, abuse, bullying, losing a job, and financial difficulty. Tragic news stories about terrorist attacks, mass shootings, and natural catastrophes are a common reality. People must learn how to deal with and get through really difficult life circumstances.

The concepts behind how individuals respond to and adjust to challenges like adversity, change, loss, and danger are referred to as resilience theory.

Even those who are tough go through stress, mental turmoil, and pain. Some individuals confuse mental toughness with resilience, but displaying resilience requires overcoming emotional anguish and suffering.

Resilience is a variable quality. People who are flexible, adaptable, and persistent may increase their resilience by altering specific attitudes and habits. According to research, kids who think they can grow their social and intellectual skills perform better and experience less stress when faced with challenges.

Building resilience is a difficult and individual process. There is no one-size-fits-all method for increasing resilience; rather, it requires a mix of internal resources and external ones. Each person is unique: Following a stressful occurrence, some people may have depression or anxiety symptoms, while others may not experience any symptoms at all.

There isn't a straightforward task list to get through adversity; resilience is the result of a variety of elements working together. In one long-term research, protective variables for depressed teenagers, such as strong familial ties, optimistic self-perceptions, and positive interpersonal relationships, were linked to robust results in early adulthood.

While everyone deals with stress and adversity differently, several protective elements help people become more resilient by enhancing their coping mechanisms and flexibility. These elements consist of:

Practical Planning Making and executing realistic strategies enables people to play to their strengths and concentrate on attainable objectives. Self-Esteem When faced with difficulty, one might avoid feeling powerless if they have a healthy sense of self and confidence in their abilities.

Coping Techniques

A person who needs to work through adversity and conquer suffering gains

empowerment from having coping and problem-solving abilities.
Skills in Communication People may seek assistance, organize resources, and take action when they can communicate simply and effectively.

Emotional Control

When facing difficulty, being able to control potentially overpowering emotions and seek support to work through them helps individuals stay focused.

According to research on the resilience hypothesis, it is critical to control a person's immediate environment and foster protective variables while addressing the demands and stresses that the person encounters. In other words, resilience is a skill that individuals may use at any time and not only in trying circumstances. It increases when individuals regularly experience various stresses, and protective elements may be fostered.

CHAPTER 2:

Resilience: Why Is It Important?

Resilient people are better able to emotionally withstand trauma, adversity, and suffering. People who are resilient make use of their assets, talents, and abilities to overcome obstacles and recover from failures.

People who lack resilience are more prone to experience overwhelming or helpless feelings and turn to negative coping mechanisms as a result (such as avoidance, isolation, and self-medication). According to one research, patients who had tried suicide had resilience scale ratings that were considerably lower than those of individuals who had never attempted suicide.

Stress, setbacks, and tough emotions are common for resilient individuals, but they manage to overcome them by drawing on their resources and enlisting the aid of their support networks. They are more able to accept and adjust to a circumstance and move on when they are resilient.

CHAPTER 3

TYPES of RESILIENCE

Although the term "resilience" is often used to refer to general adaptability and coping, it may also be classified into other sorts or categories:

- Psychological toughness
- Emotional toughness
- Physical toughness
- Community adaptability

PSYCHOLOGICAL RESILIENCE: What Is It?

The capacity to psychologically tolerate or adapt to uncertainties, difficulties, and adversity is referred to as psychological resilience. "Mental fortitude" is another name for it.

Psychologically resilient people acquire coping skills and coping mechanisms that allow them to stay composed and focused in the face of a catastrophe and recover without suffering long-term repercussions.

EMOTIONAL RESILIENCE: What Is It?

The degree to which a person can emotionally handle pressure and hardship varies. Some individuals are more or less susceptible to change by nature. A person's response to a circumstance has the power to unleash a wave of emotions.

Emotionally strong people are aware of their feelings and their motivations. Even in times of crisis, they maintain a sense of realistic optimism and are proactive in making use of both internal and external resources. They are thus able to deal with pressures and their emotions in a healthy, advantageous manner.

PHYSICAL RESILIENCE: What Is It?

Physical resiliency is the body's capacity to overcome obstacles, keep its strength and endurance, and heal swiftly and effectively. It refers to a person's capacity to carry out daily activities and bounce back after accidents, illnesses, or other physical demands.

As individuals experience medical concerns and physical stresses, research published in April 2016 in The Journal of Gerontology revealed that physical resilience plays a crucial role in healthy aging. (7)

Building physical resilience involves adopting healthy lifestyle choices, developing relationships, setting aside time for rest and recuperation, deep breathing, and taking part in pleasant activities.

COMMUNITY RESILIENCE: What Is It?

The capacity of a community to react to and bounce back from challenging circumstances, such as natural disasters, violent crimes, economic difficulties, and other challenges to their community, is referred to as community resilience.

The communities of Gilroy, California, El Paso, Texas, and Dayton, Ohio, in the wake of recent mass shootings, are real-life examples of community resilience. They also include New York City after the 9/11 terrorist attacks, Newtown, Connecticut, after the Sandy Hook Elementary School shooting, New Orleans after Hurricane Katrina, and Newtown, Connecticut, after the Sandy Hook Elementary School shooting.

Studies and Data on Resilience

The premise that specific protective resources, rather than the absence of risk factors, play a substantial influence on a person's ability to face and overcome stresses is supported by research on what fosters resilience. (8) A person's capacity for resilience may be built up and strengthened by factors such as social support, flexible coping mechanisms, and the capacity to draw on one's inner resources.

The evidence is conflicting when it comes to the concept of "natural resilience," or a person's fundamental capacity to overcome difficulty.

According to certain research, overcoming hardship with human resilience is pretty typical. This is corroborated by the finding of one research that only 5–10% of Americans who are exposed to stressful experiences go on to acquire post-traumatic stress disorder (PTSD).

However, other studies emphasize how challenging it is to investigate resilience. One specific research looked at marital loss, divorce, and unemployment and showed that the statistical model used to interpret the resilience scores had a significant impact on the outcomes. This study was published in March 2016 in the journal Perspectives on Psychological Science. The authors concluded that earlier studies may have overstated how widespread resilience is, and they made the argument that resilience may be more difficult to measure and investigate than previously believed.

CHAPTER 4

RESILIENCE TRAINING

Good news! Resilience is a skill that can be developed. People may establish social support systems or learn to reframe unfavorable beliefs, for instance.

Being resilient does not only include learning to "grin and bear it" or to "get over it." It's not about figuring out how to dodge challenges or battle against change.

By using flexibility to reframe mental patterns and learning to draw on their strengths to overcome challenges, individuals may develop resilience.

CHAPTER 5

HOW TO CREATE AND FOSTER RESILIENCE

Resilience is best understood as a process. The following actions may be taken to gradually increase resilience:

Become more self-aware. Learning more adaptive coping mechanisms begins with understanding how you generally react to stress and hardship. Understanding your talents and limitations is also part of being self-aware.

Develop your self-control abilities. Although crucial, maintaining attention amid pressure and difficulty is difficult. People who struggle with stress management might benefit from practices like mindfulness training, breathing exercises, and guided visualization.

Gain Coping Mechanisms.

Many coping mechanisms may be used to cope with difficult and stressful circumstances. They include keeping a diary, refocusing thoughts, working exercise, being outside, interacting with others, enhancing sleep hygiene, and engaging in creative activities. Boost your optimism. Optimistic people often feel more in control of their fate. Focus on what you can do when presented with a dilemma and come up with constructive, problem-solving actions to perform to increase your optimism.

strengthen connections Resilience may be greatly aided by supportive systems. Strengthen your current relationships and look for chances to start new ones.
Recognize your talents. When someone can recognize and use their abilities and talents, they feel more competent and self-assured.

How Hard Are You?

Being resilient is a temporary condition. One stressor may seem manageable and another overwhelming at the same time. When faced with difficulty, keep in mind the elements that contribute to resilience and make an effort to use them.

Resilient people often exhibit several of the following traits:

Center of Control Thinks about how you can influence events rather than outside factors.
Social Assistance Rely on your loved ones, friends, and coworkers as necessary.
Skills for Solving Issues Find strategies you may use to work on and solve an issue.

Optimism When things become difficult has faith in your capacity to manage them.
Coping Techniques Look for methods to lower anxiety and tension.
Self-care: Put your physical, mental, and emotional well-being first.

Know your talents and weaknesses as well as how to use your resources. Conditions of Health and Resilience According to studies, traits of resilience, such as strong social ties and a feeling of self-worth, are beneficial to those dealing with chronic disease.

A patient's resilience may have an impact on the course and outcome of their diseases, according to a review of the literature on resilience and chronic disease that was published in April 2015 in the journal Cogent Psychology.

CHAPTER 6

RESILIENCE AND MENTAL HEALTH

A protective factor against psychological discomfort in difficult circumstances including loss or trauma is resilience. Stress levels and depression symptoms may be better managed with its assistance. The ability to manage difficulties and adversity mentally is referred to as psychological resilience.

CHAPTER 7

THE BATTLE AGAINST RHEUMATOID ARTHRITIS

According to research, people with rheumatoid arthritis (RA) and other chronic illnesses may benefit from using behavioral and emotional techniques to build resilience. According to one research, optimism and the perception of social support enhance RA patients' quality of life.

Immunological conditions and adaptability

According to research, physical toughness might lessen the negative impact that stresses have on the immune system. According to studies, poor resilience is linked to illness progression, while strengthening resilience is linked to a higher quality of life.

Brain Damage and Willpower

In one study, patients with traumatic brain injuries who tested moderate-high on a resilience scale reported significantly fewer post-injury symptoms and better quality of life than those who tested low on resilience, according to research that was published in July 2015 in the Journal of Neurotrauma.

Diabetes Type 2 and Willpower

The Mayo Clinic claims that diabetes patients with high resilience had lower

A1C values, a sign of improved glycemic management.

Cancer and Fortitude

Resilience, particularly a person's inner resources and social support system, has been associated with better psychological and treatment-related outcomes for cancer patients, according to research that was published in the journal Frontiers in Psychiatrist

Resilience and Digestive Conditions

Gastrointestinal discomfort is usually listed as the main symptom of anxiety and depression. Resilience development may ease the tension and stress brought on by various GI problems. Low resilience was linked to increased symptoms of irritable bowel syndrome (IBS), according to research that was published in January 2018 in the journal Neurogastroenterology and Motility.

Skin Issues and Hardiness

Anxiety and stress are often present with dermatological problems. In turn, stress may cause skin diseases like eczema and psoriasis to flare up. According to studies, people who have diseases like psoriasis have indicators of lower resilience, and early interventions to increase resilience may help with symptoms and treatment of these diseases.

Resilience and Endometriosis

Endometriosis and persistent, possibly incapacitating pain have been associated in studies with negative mood, anxiety, and decreased resilience. Resilience may have a significant role in minimizing the negative consequences on social, mental, and physical well-being.

Children's Resilience

Growing up presents kids with a variety of difficulties, from beginning school and meeting new friends to traumatic, harmful events like bullying and abuse.

According to the American Psychological Association, "building resilience" may help our children handle stress and emotions of worry and uncertainty. "Building resilience" is the capacity to adapt successfully to adversity, trauma, tragedy, danger, or even substantial sources of stress (APA).

The 7 Cs strategy focuses primarily on fostering resilience in children and teenagers. For young people to manage circumstances successfully, it identifies competence, confidence, connection, character, contribution, coping, and control as necessary abilities.

Parents may promote resilience in their kids by modeling good habits and ideas. The APA offers the following 10 suggestions for fostering youth resilience:

Encourage social interaction
Allowing kids to assist others can benefit them.

Maintain a regular schedule

Take pauses from stressful situations
instill self-care
Set sensible objectives.
Maintain an optimistic view of yourself
Maintaining perspective
Encourage self-reflection
Accept that life is full of change.
There is no one-size-fits-all approach to helping young people develop resilience. Parents may think about speaking with a counselor, psychologist, or other mental health specialists if their kid seems overburdened or distressed both at school and home.

CHAPTER 8

Does Resilience Vary by Gender?

Men and women may react to hardship and trauma in different ways, according to research on resilience and gender. However, the outcomes have been mixed.

Women have typically fared better than males in terms of lifespan and survival amid emergencies like famines and epidemics. Researchers discovered that women outlived males by six months to four years, even while total life expectancy increased, according to a paper published in January 2018 in Proceedings of the National Academy of Sciences. (19)

However, research has shown that women are almost twice as likely as males to get PTSD after a severe incident. Uncertainty over the cause of the gender gap suggests that it may have something to do with coping mechanisms for trauma.

Female Resilience

When faced with difficulties and misfortune, resilience helps men and women alike. However, women also rely on resilience to get through challenges like workplace discrimination, sexual harassment, and domestic abuse that are more often put in their path.

According to one research, women who faced workplace discrimination relied on masculine traits, mentorship, and intrinsic motivating factors to overcome challenges.

Male Resilience

Men and women who are resilient are less likely to suffer from mental illnesses like sadness and anxiety.

According to research, males who lack resilience are far more likely to experience severe depression after the death of a partner.

The research, which was published in September 2018 in the journal The Gerontologist, also revealed that men with high levels of resilience did not have any extra depression symptoms after a loss and that their general well-being was nearly identical to that of their married counterparts.

Another research that looked particularly at perceived sources of stress and resiliency among African American males and was published in the journal Progress in Community Health Partnerships in 2014 revealed that most men found support for resiliency via family and religion.

CHAPTER 9

ADAPTABILITY IN CAREGIVING

The stress of providing care for someone, such as an elderly relative or a loved one who has a chronic illness, may be very high and harm the caregiver's health.

According to research, social support has a critical moderating role in carers' resilience. Along with doctors and social professionals, family members and friends may also provide such assistance.

To lessen the load on caregivers, one research, which was published in January 2018 in the journal BMC Psychiatry, emphasized that medical practitioners should assist in locating dependable family members and friends.

Inspirational Sayings and Quotes to Boost Your Resilience

People may be encouraged to be resilient in a variety of ways. Even something as basic as a motivational saying may be uplifting. Tattoos are a surprising example of a form of expression that may convey a story of resiliency and inspire others.

CHAPTER 10

How Does Resilience Affect Recovery?

There are a lot more factors involved in maintaining soberness than just avoiding drugs or alcohol. Long-term sobriety will eventually result from addressing underlying problems like low self-esteem, trauma, or a lack of coping mechanisms.

Recovery and resiliency go hand in hand. Long-term addiction treatment, creating a sober support network, and working on life skills like resilience can all help you stay clean and make it easier for you to deal with problems that may otherwise cause you to relapse.

Any recovering person who lacks resilience is significantly more likely to relapse since they will inevitably encounter difficult situations that will test their sobriety and may not have the resources to deal with them. Working through difficult situations may often mean the difference between long-term sobriety and relapse.

10 Techniques for Increasing Resilience in Sobriety

You may attempt to build resilience in your everyday recovery in a variety of ways.

2 Here are 10 techniques to build resilience in recovery, regardless of how long you have been clean.

Establish Sober Ties.
A sober living program, IOP, or aftercare program will provide you the chance to continue your addiction therapy and give you numerous chances to build sober, uplifting, and healthy connections in recovery. Attending AA or NA meetings regularly is another excellent approach to meeting sober people.

Start seeing difficulties as chances to become better.
Consider how these hurdles might help you individually develop rather than seeing relapse, financial concerns, or relationship issues as failures. Although there are many difficult situations in life, how we handle them makes all the difference.

Recognize that you can't control everything.

You will never be able to control everything in life, but that's good. Resilience can help you deal with stress and discover strategies to get through challenging situations as a healthy, sober person in recovery without succumbing to the urge to use drugs or alcohol as a crutch.

Set up your objectives and work toward them every day.
Even if they are modest, having objectives to strive towards is crucial. You may prioritize daily and weekly objectives like making your bed every morning, practicing meditation for 10 minutes each day, or seeing your sober coach once a week.

Make a Move.

Instead of isolating yourself or adopting a victim mindset while facing difficult situations, take proactive steps to address the problem or get through it. Being proactive can aid you in overcoming emotions of failure and self-loathing that could trigger a relapse.

actively look for chances for personal development.
Even in the middle of a challenging circumstance, consider how you may benefit from it. Even while it's not always simple to see the bright side, challenging circumstances like debt, strained relationships, or the death of a loved one can provide chances for development and healing.

Have confidence in your skills and talents.

It helps a lot to have faith in your abilities to maintain sobriety and have a healthy, happy life. Even though it takes time to build confidence, being around encouraging, sober people will also teach you how to trust yourself and be confident in your capacity to handle issues, conquer challenges, and maintain sobriety.

Keep a level head.

It's simple to exaggerate things, particularly when drugs and alcohol are impairing your judgment. Every feeling is acceptable in sobriety, but how you choose to respond will decide whether you manage to remain clean or succumb to the urge to relapse.

Self-care is advisable.

In a life of recovery, taking care of your body and mind has numerous advantages and will make sure you're ready to deal with challenges in sobriety. Making self-care a priority while in recovery can also offer you more energy to assist others, increase your productivity, promote self-discovery, and assist you in keeping your attention on the present rather than on the past.

Encourage spirituality.

In both good and difficult times, spiritual activities like yoga and meditation may help you regain hope and tranquility. These techniques may also help you stay grounded and get rid of any unresolved negative feelings that are preventing you from living your sobriety to the fullest.

How Resilience Training in a Sober Living Program Can Help You in Recovery

Programs for sober living provide several advantages for those in recovery who lack fortitude or other life skills.

Opportunities for social interaction with other sober persons are offered via sober living programs.
To assist you in starting a new life, sober living programs provide useful recovery support services like the job and educational assistance.

Sober living programs demand devotion to a life in recovery, a set schedule, and healthy routines. Programs for sober life provide accountability.

In rehabilitation, sober living programs promote accountability and personal development.

Call Eudaimonia Recovery Homes to learn more about our sober living programs for adults in Houston, Austin, and Colorado Springs if you're finding it difficult to maintain sobriety and lack resilience.

www.ingramcontent.com/pod-product-compliance
Lightning Source LLC
La Vergne TN
LVHW020525160826
845677LV00015B/3905
* 9 7 9 8 3 6 4 5 6 8 9 9 1 *